Book/DVD

Percussive Acoustic

by Chris Woods

ISBN 978-1-4584-5964-0

HAL•LEONARD®
CORPORATION

7777 W. BLUEMOUND RD. P.O. BOX 13819 MILWAUKEE, WI 53213

In Australia Contact:
Hal Leonard Australia Pty. Ltd.
4 Lentara Court
Cheltenham, Victoria, 3192 Australia
Email: ausadmin@halleonard.com.au

Visit Hal Leonard Online at
www.halleonard.com

ABOUT THE AUTHOR

Chris Woods is one the UK's leading instrumental acoustic guitarists, described as "changing the perceived boundaries of the acoustic guitar." As well as being a creative composer and a performer with a rigorous touring schedule, he has a passion for teaching and sharing his creative approach to playing.

www.chriswoodsgroove.co.uk

Table of Contents

Introduction

This book can completely change the way you play and approach the guitar. Designed to promote originality and style through a friendly offering of some fresh perspectives, *Percussive Acoustic Guitar* takes you step by step through several exciting techniques. With practice, you'll master the art of body percussion, string slapping, right-hand tapping, slapped harmonics, and much more. The exercises are designed to help you grasp the techniques and then implement them in your own playing, whether you are a professional singer-songwriter, a happy busker, or a virtuoso instrumental player. This book is accessible to all.

Each technique has been given its own dedicated chapter, and every one is packed full of exercises that will take you from the basics right up to an advanced level—all in manageable bite-sized chunks. Additionally, each exercise is preceded by its very own warm up, which will help prepare you for the task at hand. Finally, we conclude with four full pieces that bring it all together.

The wonderful thing about percussive playing is the way it can enhance any style. These techniques can be used to spice up a "strum along" or to bring the most in-depth guitar solo to life. Once you get going, you'll wonder how ever you lived without it. Good luck!

Plugging In

In order to use some of the body percussion techniques in this book in a live situation that requires a PA, amplifier, or similar, you will need to think about how you receive and amplify your guitar's sound. A microphone will successfully pick up all of your body percussion techniques and the more standard ways of playing, however, in a live situation, only using a microphone can be problematic with feedback, and of course, the issue of not being able to move freely.

Most contemporary acoustic players opt to use a pickup. Pickups come in many shapes and sizes, but the principal remains the same: they are designed to "pick up" the sound of your guitar. Unfortunately, many aren't designed to pick up body percussion on the guitar, so your percussive hits might sound like faint knocks, rather than powerful, percussive "thwacks!"—or even worse, you might not hear anything at all. However, there is an ever increasing range of pickup solutions.

Often blending a standard piezo or magnetic pickup with an internal microphone may give you the most practical solution. But still, the simple addition of a standard external condenser microphone alongside a standard pickup will do the trick. Ultimately, in the same way as you should approach the techniques in this book, experiment and be creative. Live sound is an exciting world with countless options that go far beyond pickups and microphones; it can seriously enhance your sound and even be the driving force behind your own signature style. So get experimenting, because the sky is the limit!

THE BASICS: Getting a Feel for It All

The following examples are designed to give you a taste of the fundamental percussive techniques. To make it easy, they all use two simple standard chords and are based around a very similar groove.

String Slapping

String slapping is the most common percussive technique, appearing in countless genres. Here's how to do it...

Use your thumb (on your picking hand) to lazily slap against the strings; the movement mainly comes from your wrist. Essentially, you are just letting your thumb come to rest against the lower strings. The harder you do it, the louder it gets! The sound created is a dead, percussive "tick," and often the strings bounce off the frets if done relatively strongly. Here's a short example, in which the slap is notated with an X.

☞ **TIP:** Keep doing this until it's completely natural. I promise it will help in the long run!

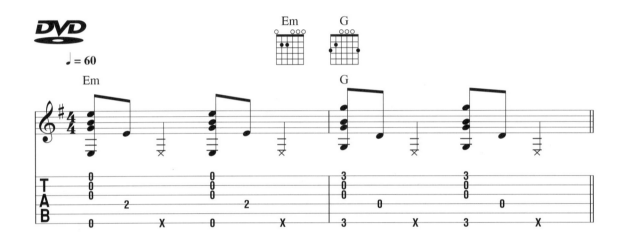

Body Percussion

When we say *body percussion,* we're referring to the body of the guitar—not your body! Arguably originating from flamenco music, this is a really great-sounding technique that sounds and looks complicated, but it's not rocket science. The guitar is a big resonating wooden box, so it makes a lot of sense to hit it, right? We're essentially mimicking what a drummer might do, but a little less violently. (Don't break your guitar!) Here's how you do it...

If you spend five minutes tapping on the body of the guitar, you'll discover a world of different tones. But for now, let's stick with two sounds: the "kick drum" and "snare drum" (just like on a drum kit!).

KICK: It's best to use your thumb here or even the heel of your hand. Knock the main part of the body (just below the bridge) and try to create the lowest tone possible.

SNARE: This is a little more challenging. We're using the fingers and the inside of your knuckles to rap against the side of the guitar. It's similar to how a Djembe drummer would achieve a rim shot. Aim for the side of the guitar, just below the strap button, and don't hit so hard that it hurts!

☞ **TIP:** Remember each guitar sounds totally different, so experiment with using different parts of the body until you're happy with the tone.

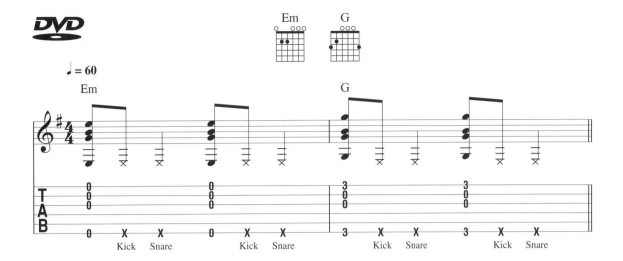

Tapping

Though it's been made more famous by electric players like Eddie Van Halen, on an acoustic, the *tapping* technique can sound melodic and very percussive at the same time. It also opens up a whole new world of note choices, too. Here's how to do it...

Put simply, you're using your picking hand to hammer-on and pull-off. I tend to use my middle finger, as it usually seems to be the strongest. Simply hammer-on your picking-hand finger to the desired note. Then, pull your (picking) hand off so that a lower note on that string rings out. Usually, the tapping technique is combined with traditional fret hand hammer-ons and pull-offs, creating long streams of notes. In the following music example, the tap is notated with a "+" (above the notation staff) and a "T" (above the tablature staff).

TIP: There's no need to attack the string from a great height. Make sure the movement comes from your finger; as your finger muscles get stronger, the note will ring more clearly.

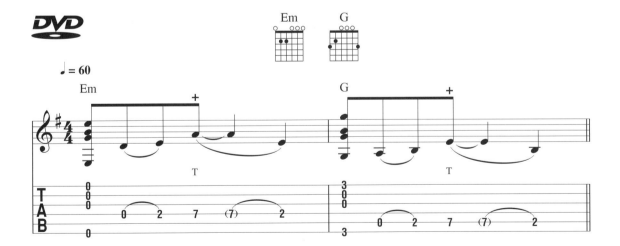

Harmonics

There are many ways to play *harmonics,* and we have a whole chapter dedicated to them. In the meantime, however, all you really need to understand is how to make the basic sound. They have an ethereal quality and can really stand out in a piece. Here's how to do it...

We're going to try two different approaches here: first, a standard natural harmonic for those beginners, and then a "slapped" harmonic—both within the same exercise.

NATURAL HARMONICS

Rest the first finger of your fretting hand lightly over the 12th fret of strings 4–1. You should only touch the string; don't push it down to the fretboard. Make sure you are directly over the fret wire. Pluck these four strings at the same time—either strummed or fingerpicked—and move your fretting hand away immediately, giving the strings room to vibrate.

SLAPPED HARMONICS

Using your middle finger of your picking hand, "slap" across the 12th fret as an alternative to the previous method. Precision and accuracy isn't the key here, but fluidity of motion is. Make sure you bounce off the fret quickly, and don't be afraid to give it a good whack. The slapped harmonics are indicated with an "S" above the tab staff.

> **TIPS:** Harmonics are temperamental things, so if you're stuck, make sure you're giving the strings room to vibrate. Remember, you should only lightly touch the strings; don't push them down!

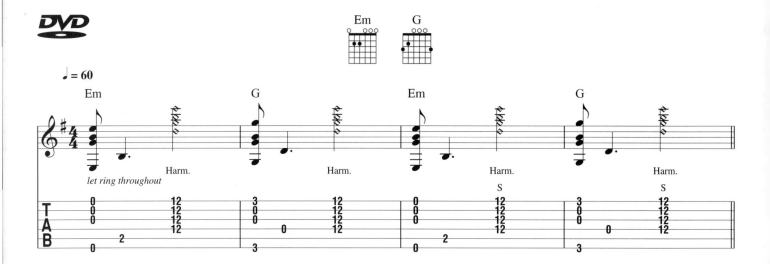

Alternate Tunings

Retuning your guitar to an open chord—or even just tweaking one string—can completely change the sound of the guitar and the possibilities available. It lends itself well to percussive playing, and having all those open strings available in the song's key enables you to play a melody with your fretting hand while your picking hand plays body percussion. Also, having slackened strings gives the guitar a real percussive quality in itself. There are endless options when it comes to alternate tunings; some players even change their string gauges to make the craziest of tunings possible. I would recommend using an electronic tuner at first to avoid string breakages! Here are a few alternate tuning ideas for you:

DROP D TUNING (D–A–D–G–B–E): There's nothing major here. We just drop the low E string to a D. Try strumming a D major chord in this tuning and then experiment with simple melodies while the open D string plods away in support.

DADGAD: A seriously popular tuning, DADGAD is very popular in the folk world. There's lots of scope for open and moveable chord shapes.

DROP C TUNING (C–A–D–G–B–E): This is just the same as the first tuning, but with the low E dropped down to C. "That's low!" I hear you cry. Well it is, but John Mayer's "Neon" will demonstrate how effective it can be!

CSUS2 TUNING (C–G–C–G–C–D): This is a strange tuning, but my favorite! It creates an open Csus2 chord and enables you to play in octaves very easily.

BM7 TUNING (B–F♯–B–F♯–A–D): This is the lowest tuning mentioned so far, but it's worth at least venturing there once. To get low down to B, you really should have gauge 12 strings or thicker; anything lower will flop around a bit too much.

E–A–C♯–F♯–B–E: This one's a bit of a wild card, but it's easy to get to and lets you play in the A Lydian mode till your heart's content!

☞ **TIP:** Experimenting is the key, so why not find your own?

A NOTE ON PICKING

We all have different approaches to strumming or fingerpicking, and it's impossible to say which approach or system is best. There is certainly no such thing as a wrong approach. It's worth noting that the vast majority of the following pieces have been written with a specific system in mind: Thumb for strings 6, 5, and 4, first finger for string 3, second finger for string 2, and third finger for string 1. That's how I normally do it, but this book is all about creativity, so whether you use a plectrum or thumb and one finger, you'll still have hours of fun with every exercise!

CHAPTER ONE: String Slapping

Mastering string slapping will open up a whole new world of percussive possibilities in your playing. In this chapter, we'll look at the basic muted percussive slap and eventually move on to a "slap bass"-style approach. Both are seriously percussive and very effective. You'll have it all mastered in no time; just stay relaxed, and remember the movements should be natural.

The Snare Drum Slap

THE WARM UP

Here's a nice simple warm up. Let the side of your thumb come to rest against the lower strings. Don't worry about being too precise; even though the "X" is notated on the E string, we are simply aiming for the lower strings. We want a muted sound, so once you make contact with the string, don't lift the thumb away too quickly.

Note that we're slapping on the 2nd and 4th beat of the bar (just like a snare drum would usually play). Try counting "1, slap, 3, slap" in your head to help you. Don't move on until you can slap confidently and freely on beats 2 and 4.

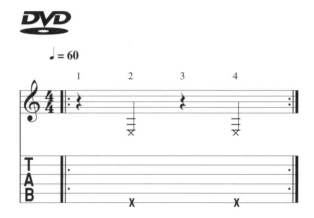

THE EXERCISE

BARS 1–4: Count "1 and 2 and 3 and 4 and" to help you keep time. The pattern is very repetitive: a simple down-and-up strumming pattern with a slap thrown in. Notice how the string slap replaces where a downstroke would be.

BARS 5–8: Here we move to fingerpicking and add an extra note (the high E played after the string slap). The open low E string is played very quickly after the string slap. Try to play it as you pull away from the string slap in one smooth movement.

BARS 9–12: Things become a lot busier here! It's all just a repeated pattern, so don't panic and take your time.

The Offbeat Slap

THE WARM UP

Slapping on the offbeat can really make a rhythm feel far livelier. Put simply, we are slapping in between the beat, so just count "1 slap 2 slap 3 slap 4 slap." The result should be a driving rhythm reminiscent of a Johnny Cash song!

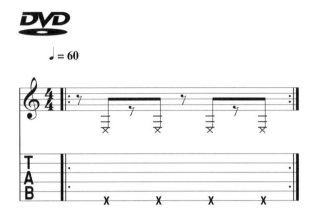

THE EXERCISE

BARS 1–8: This is a basic repeated pattern, so focus on that offbeat slap and how the pattern works.

BARS 9–13: Things are a little more demanding here with you having to play far more notes on either side of the slap. It's worth mastering this separately before you try to glue it all together. Once again, notice the pattern: in this case, it really only lasts half a bar before it repeats; use the low E string as your signal for the repetition. Try counting "1 e and a, 2 e and a, 3 e and a, 4 e and a," slapping on the "and."

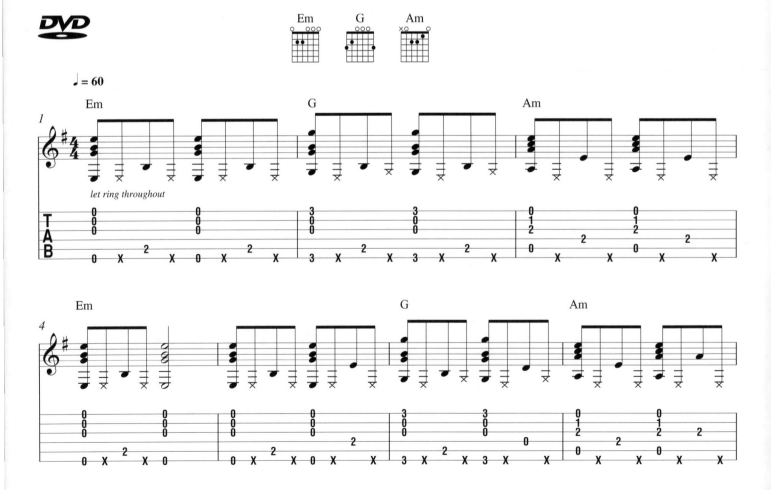

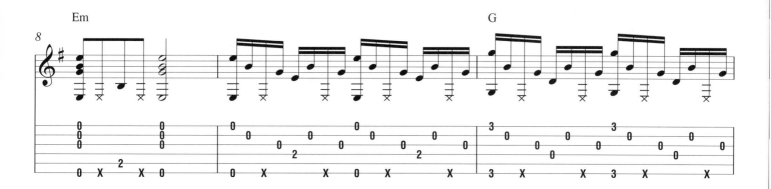

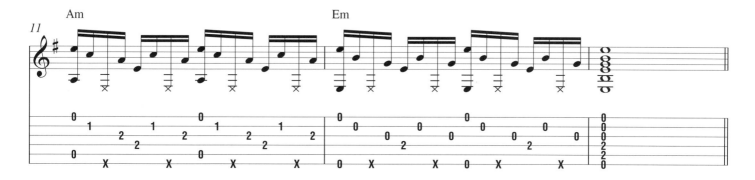

The Thumb Work Out

THE WARM UP

We're now giving our thumb a bit more work, with the simple addition of an upstroke. Play the first note down, then slap the string and quickly follow this with an upstroke of the thumb, finishing with another downstroke to start the pattern over. Take this one note at a time and accept the fact that it may take a while for it to become a natural movement.

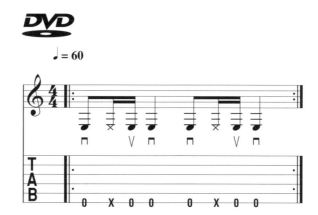

THE EXERCISE

BARS 1–5: Focus on getting a nice, natural groove on one chord before you move on, making sure you are consistent with the downstrokes and upstrokes of the thumb.

BARS 5–9: The pattern has changed slightly, but never fear; just look at the tab for a moment and notice that we've simply created a longer phrase! If you're feeling confident, this is the ideal time to try throwing in a strum or two in place of the fingerpicked notes.

Slap Bass Style

THE WARM UP

Okay, so this is new territory. We are now trying to slap the bass strings like a slap bass player might. We'll be slapping the string (notated with an "S") in a similar sideways motion as before, but this time there is one major difference: we are "bouncing" off the string so it can vibrate. Finally, we are popping the fourth string with our first finger (notated with a "P"). Pull up on the string and allow it to snap back against the fretboard with lots of attack.

If this technique is completely new to you, it may take hours to get a handle on it (or even get a sound). Try and attempt the following warm up in 15-minute bursts with a very short break in between to avoid building tension. Master each bar before you attempt the next, keep it funky, and never give up!

BAR 1: Slap the E string, but imagine you are bouncing a ball. Strike the string and then pull away. Make sure the movement is coming from your wrist—almost as if you are turning a key in a door. If the note isn't ringing out, you are probably not moving away quickly enough; remember to bounce.

BAR 2: This is exactly the same as bar 1, but notice how the notes are now shorter. We are now "killing" each note by touching the relevant string with our fretting hand to stop it from vibrating.

BAR 3: We are now slapping the A string. To help avoid hitting the E string, try using the palm of your picking hand (or even a fretting-hand finger) to mute the E. Don't forget to kill the note afterward with your fretting hand.

BAR 4: Here we introduce the "pop" (notated with a "P"). Use your first finger to literally hook under the string and pull up, releasing it to snap against the fretboard. (A fretted note can be killed by taking the pressure off after the note has been played.)

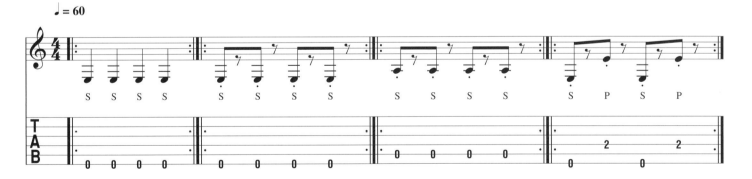

THE EXERCISE

BARS 1–4: The key thing to creating a good sound here is to remember to kill each note after you've played it with your fretting hand. Just gently touch the strings enough to stop the vibrations. This will help tighten up the overall sound.

BARS 5–6: We are now throwing in a hammer-on on the second note of the bar. When combined with the pop technique, this should sound really funky. Focus on getting the timing right.

Slapping with Two Hands

THE WARM UP

If you've been struggling when using your fretting hand to kill the notes, and/or the slap movement is not becoming natural, now is the time to go back and try approaching things again, but much more slowly. Take as long as you need on each exercise before you move on, stay relaxed, and enjoy it.

We're now taking the slap bass concept one step further and actually making a percussive sound with our fretting hand. Rather than just touching the string with our fretting hand to kill the note, we tap or slap the strings (it takes a bit of getting used to!) to create a percussive noise.

In this warm up, we are slapping the first note with our picking hand, then tapping or slapping a percussive sound with our fretting hand. Next, we slap a muted note with our picking hand (we'll mute this with our fretting hand, so just leave it there from the previous fret hand slap) and finally pop string 4 with our picking hand. Phew! This fret hand tap/slap works brilliantly when combined with muted strumming too.

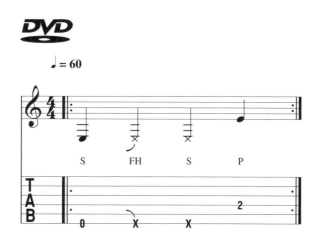

THE EXERCISE

This exercise is basically a quicker version of the warm up, and we make our way to the A string to repeat the same pattern. The key here is to practice very slowly, making sure all the notes are evenly spaced. If you get it wrong, try it slower the next time until you get it. It's that simple!

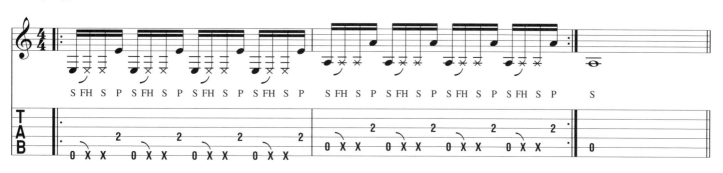

The Hammered Slap

THE WARM UP

Slap bass players don't just slap open or muted notes; they use them all. In this warm up, we are naturally progressing from the previous exercise. Rather than creating a muted note with your fretting hand, we're now hammering onto the 3rd fret and then slapping that note.

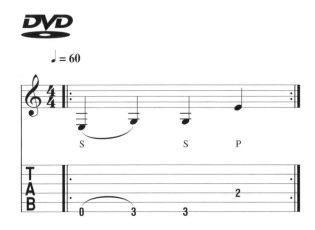

THE EXERCISE

This is just the same as the warm up, but we've squeezed the same phrase in four times to each bar. Don't rush; just gradually build up to the right speed.

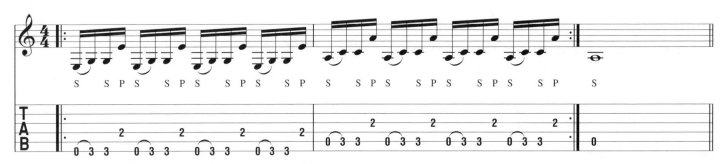

Muted Pop

THE WARM UP

Muting your popped note is, in principal, the same as muting your slapped note; simply use your fretting hand to mute the relevant string. Spend some time finding the best area to rest your hand.

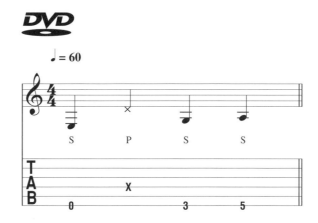

THE EXERCISE

This example introduces the muted pop and also brings in most of the techniques from the previous few exercises, including hammer-ons and muted slaps.

CHAPTER 2: Body Percussion

Arguably the most exciting element of percussive guitar playing, body percussion is certainly the technique that gets an audience's attention. My advice would be to use it sparingly in your playing. The guitar is a naturally percussive instrument, but there is a fine line between being a creative guitarist and just trying to play the drums on your guitar! Be thoughtful and creative; the whole body of the guitar can be used. We'll be focusing on some specific areas, but remember that each guitar is different, so don't feel that you have to play in exactly the same place. Just pay attention to the rhythms, use this book as inspiration, and let your musical ear decide what is best.

The Basic Beat

THE WARM UP

It can be very confusing to read tablature with body percussion squeezed in. To make it easier, we've added a second line of music specifically for guitar body percussion. But don't worry; you don't have to be able to read music well. We'll only be using two notes on this staff. All you have to remember is that the kick drum sound is the lower note, and the snare drum sound is the higher note.

BAR 1: To make the kick drum sound, try using either the side of your thumb or even the heel of your hand against the body of the guitar somewhere between the strap button and the bridge. The goal is to create a low, bassy sound.

BAR 2: To make the snare sound, tap or rap the side of the guitar with the back of your knuckles just below the strap lock. We're trying to create a higher-pitched sound here. Spend as much time as you need honing and experimenting with your technique to create the best possible sound.

BAR 3: Here we're alternating between the two so you can get used to the feel of it.

BAR 4: And here's the full beat. Try counting "1, 2, 3 and 4" to help you get the rhythm. This beat is played in countless pop songs.

THE EXERCISE

Okay, so now you can see you have two lines of music together: the guitar tablature with notation (for your picking and strumming), and the body percussion line for your raps and taps! Simply read each line together.

BARS 1–2: Strum your chord down and up for beats "1 and 2 and," follow with a very basic kick on beat 3, and finish with the snare on beat 4.

BARS 3–4: This is the same as the previous bars, except for the addition of an extra upstroke in bar 3.

BARS 5–8: Notice the introduction of a double kick drum sound and the use of the extra upstroke from bar 3. Count "3 and 4 and" or "kick, kick, snare, strum" to help you.

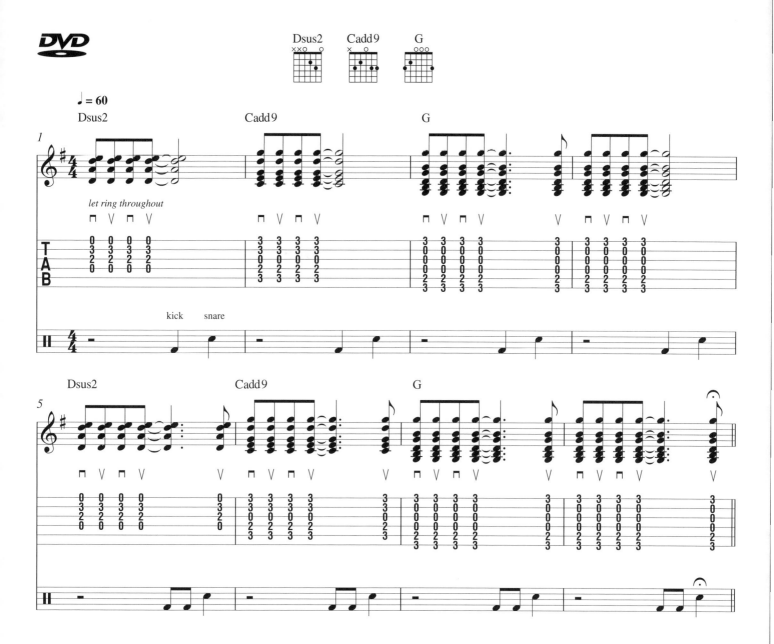

Funkin' It Up!

THE WARM UP

There are two key elements that help make something funky: leaving space and employing syncopation—i.e., playing on the offbeats.

BAR 1: We are playing our standard rock beat, except we are missing the 3rd beat. Try counting "1, 2, rest and 4."

BAR 2: Here we're adding in the "and" or offbeat after the 4th beat. So now count "1, 2, rest and 4 and."

BAR 3: The final kick drum has now been moved even closer to beat 4, on the second 16th note. This makes things sound a little more like a hip-hop beat. Try counting "1, 2, rest and 4 e."

THE EXERCISE

There's nothing too scary here, although it's worth spending a bit of time getting the picking pattern for the chords right before you attempt the whole thing. The only tricky part is that the body percussion changes half way, so just refer back to the warm up if you get stuck.

Working Together

THE WARM UP

Coordinating your left and right hand is crucial in taking your percussive playing further. This might mean you play notes at the same time as a percussive hit, or even, as in this example, just playing notes on either side of a percussive sound. Either way, it's important to approach percussive guitar playing with both hands working in harmony!

To help you through the warm up, here's a bit of a step-by-step walkthrough for the first bar:

▶ Strum a G chord with an open low E string.

▶ Hammer your second finger onto fret 3.

▶ Play a kick drum sound.

▶ Followed with another hammer-on to fret 3
(or "fret hand tap," as we don't pick the string again).

▶ Follow with a snare and kick.

▶ Finally, add another fret hand tap on fret 3.

Phew! That's a lot to take in! Take this very, very slowly at first. You are basically tapping with your fret hand onto fret 3 in between the percussive sounds. You're not playing percussion and notes at the same time, but the two hands are working alternately. The second bar is just to give you a feel for the picking pattern. The main exercise will be double the tempo, so practice this until it is completely natural!

THE EXERCISE

This exercise is essentially the two bars of the warm up glued together, except that we are now introducing the same sort of pattern within several chords. Just take your time to look at the tab and recognize the patterns. In the final bar, there's a short riff on string 5 that conforms to the same rhythm and idea; the notes are close to either side of the percussive hits.

Rolling Around and All at the Same Time

THE WARM UP

In this warm up, the beat is very similar to the previous exercise, except we are now adding three very fast hits on the snare (or side of the body) while also playing notes and percussion simultaneously.

BAR 1: Play the kick drum sound on beat 2, and then follow this with your snare drum "roll." To play the roll, simply tap your fingers in quick succession. Start with your third finger, then place down your second, and then your first. It's almost as if you were rolling your fingers on a desk out of boredom! Finally, finish with yet another kick drum sound.

BAR 2: The rhythm is slightly different here. Notice how we've added another snare drum sound at the end of the bar. Most significantly, however, is the fact that we're playing notes at the same time. Unfortunately, these types of rhythms always look a bit scary in notation, so it's really worth listening to the DVD here. It will sound very familiar to you.

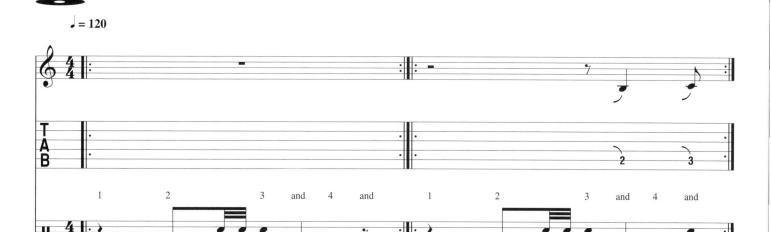

THE EXERCISE

If you managed to work your way through the warm up, this will be nice and easy. The only difference is that we've added a strummed chord. Simple!

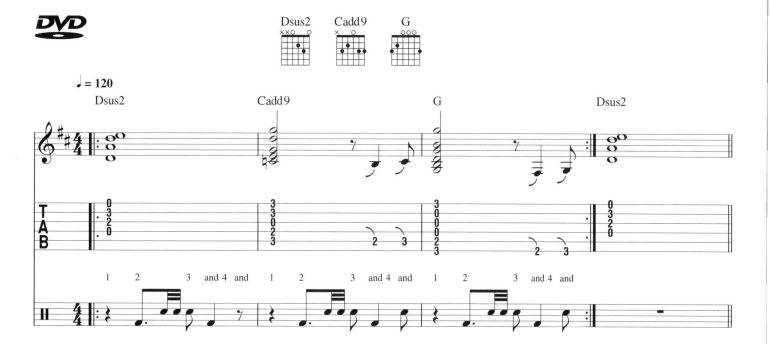

Moving Up

THE WARM UP

The past few exercises should have given you a good feel for the end of the guitar; now it's time to move to the top of the guitar. We're still only working with two sounds: the top/side of the guitar in line with your (fretting hand) shoulder, and the front of the guitar just above the sound hole towards the neck.

Play the top/side with your thumb using a downwards motion and the front side with the back of your knuckles or fingers. The movements should be almost exactly the same as in previous exercises.

The top/side (played with your thumb) will be the lower note in the music, and the front of the guitar (played with fingers) will be the higher note. In this warm up, we are playing a quick run of beats, alternating between kick and snare one after the other. Work on making this a fluid movement—almost as if you were strumming.

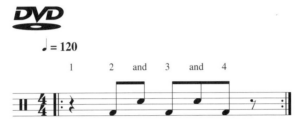

THE EXERCISE

The first three chords use the rhythm that we just learned in the warm up. The final bars leave out the third percussive beat. The key to making this musical is to experiment with dynamics. Try playing the first few notes of the percussive part much softer or emphasize one particular kick or snare.

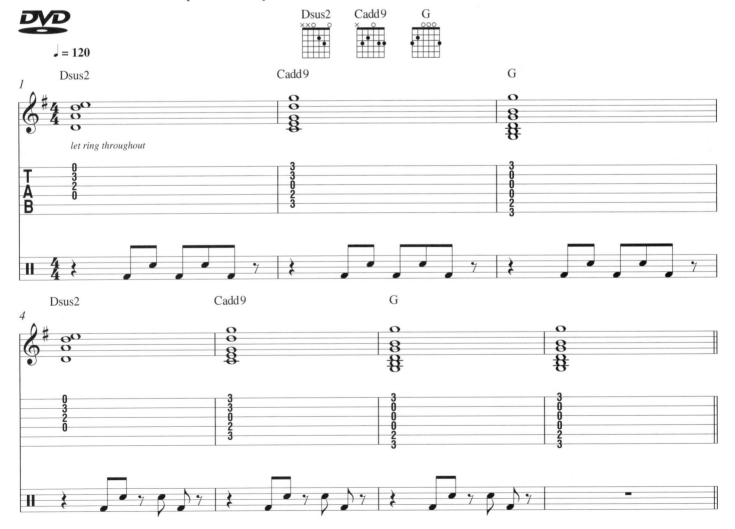

Moving Down and Mixing It Up

THE WARM UP

We are on the move again, this time to the bottom of the guitar. Your kick drum sound will be on the scratch plate (pick guard), and your snare sound will be on the bottom/side of the guitar. (You may get best results when wearing a strap, as this will give you more of the guitar to play with.) If you don't have a scratch plate, aim for the same area, but be warned that it will likely affect the finish of your guitar!

The scratch plate will be the lower note (kick), and the bottom/side will be the higher note (snare) in the music. Here's a step-by-step breakdown for the warm up:

▶ Roll your fingers—3, 2, 1—on the scratch plate. Trying doing this with your nails, as they can help create a more defined sound (be careful of marking your guitar though!).

▶ Play a simple single kick drum sound with your thumb on the scratch plate.

▶ Play a snare sound by hitting the bottom/side of the guitar.

▶ Finally, slap the strings (notice it's an "X" in the tab). A standard string slap will work well; alternatively, using your whole hand can create a really bass-heavy sound.

THE EXERCISE

This is the same as the warm up with a strummed chord at the beginning and end of the bar.

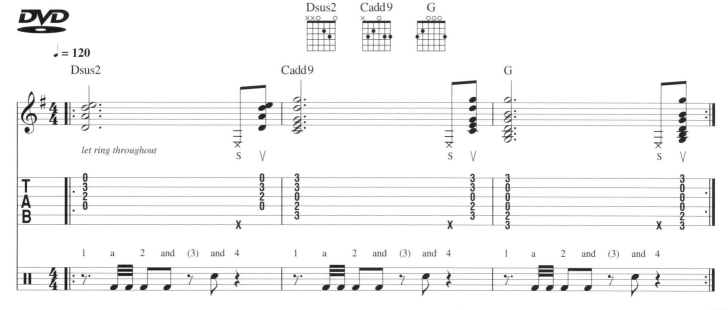

Fret Hand Percussion

THE WARM UP

It's time to start using your fret hand for percussive hits. It might seem crazy, but being able to play percussion with two hands will result in a whole new world of groove possibilities, and it's not as hard as you might think.

This exercise uses slightly different chords than the other exercises in this chapter. This is because, in order to free your fret hand up easily, we need to use chords with lots of open strings. When you begin to incorporate things like slapped harmonics, and particularly alternate tunings, this technique will really start to shine. In the meantime, let's just get a feel for it.

Notice that "FH" is written above the last snare drum beat. This indicates a "Fret Hand" snare beat. When you see this, simply rap the side of the guitar with the back of your knuckles in the same way as you have played a snare sound in previous exercises—this time with your fretting hand. Aim for the side of the guitar just below the neck.

The other previous kick drum and snare drum beats can be played anywhere on the guitar, but for now, let's use the end of the guitar, just like we were using in the first few examples of this chapter.

THE EXERCISE

We are now using an Em and Asus2 for the chord sequence. Notice how the notes are far shorter than in the warm up; make sure you build up to this and use the numbers above the bars to help you count through it. Pay attention to the upstroke after the string slap to help things flow nicely. This is significantly trickier than the warm up, but practice will make perfect.

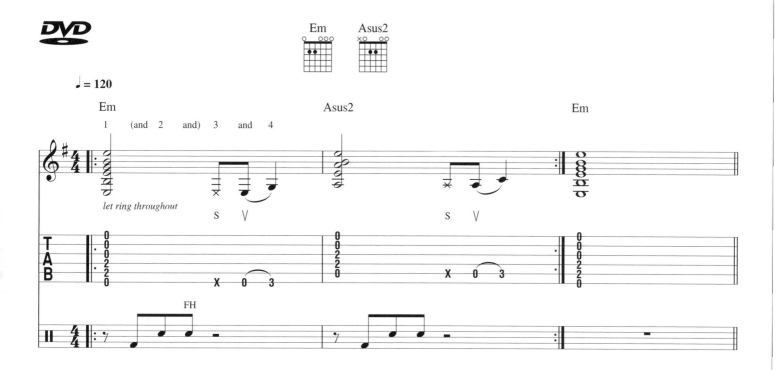

CHAPTER 3: Tapping

Hammer and Tap

THE WARM UP

Using two hands to play notes and chords is quite logical when you think about it. Piano players do it, and it works pretty well for them. It may take a while for this to become natural, but before long, you'll be tapping all over the fretboard without a care in the world. The effect is percussive, but it also gives you more options melodically and physically.

The actual process of tapping is just like a hammer-on or pull-off, except we're using the picking hand. Feel free to try using different fingers, although I tend to favor my middle finger. Simply tap down your finger onto the note in one sharp movement and hold it there while the note rings out. Here's a step-by-step breakdown for the first bar:

▶ Pluck the open B string.

▶ Now hammer on to the 1st fret with your fretting hand.

▶ Next, tap onto the 5th fret with your picking hand.

▶ Then pull your tapping finger off to the note on the 1st fret.
(Note that you need to be fretting this note before you pull off the tapping finger!)

Notice that your picking hand only plucks once!

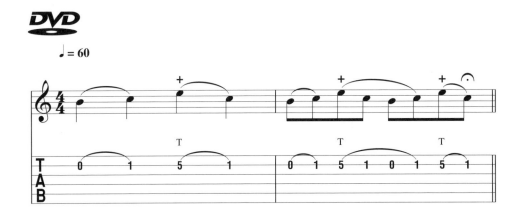

THE EXERCISE

Here we're blending chords with tapping. Give the chord a confident strum before working your way through the tapped pattern. Note that it will be easier to strum around the fretboard area, since you'll need to be there for the tapping. The chord should still ring out while you tap, resulting in a nice full sound.

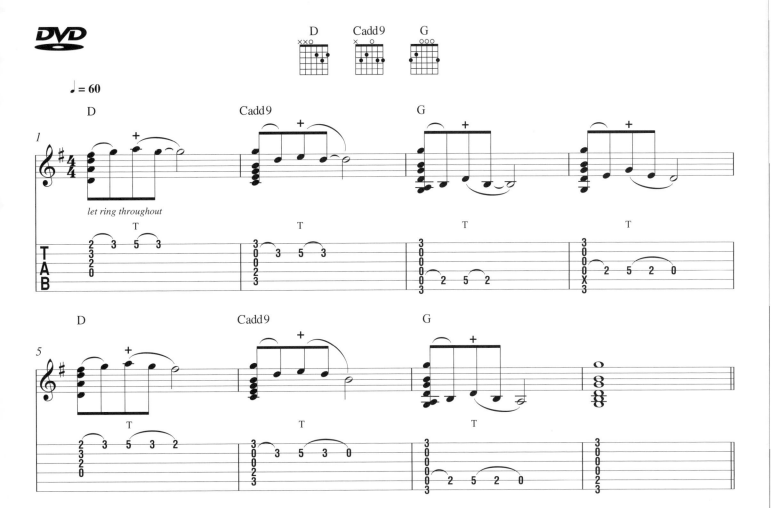

Sliding Around

THE WARM UP

With your fretting hand, it's very common to slide up or down in one smooth movement. Here, we're sliding our tapping finger around after tapping a note. At the end of the bar, we pull off back to the 1st fret, where your fretting hand will be.

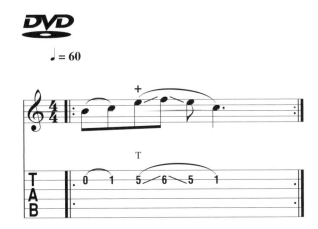

THE EXERCISE

This is very similar to the first exercise, except the chords have changed, and we are using a slide. Spend some time making the movements flow, and keep your chord fretted for as long as possible. This might not be as percussive as the body percussion, but rhythm is still the key!

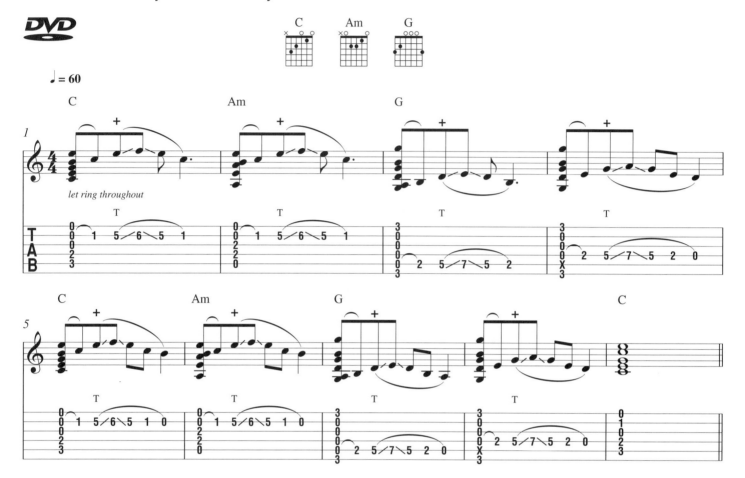

So Where Do All These Notes Come from Then?

THE WARM UP

This book is all about giving you inspiration. It's all good knowing how to tap, but what happens if you want to write something of your own? Which notes do you use? How do you find the right note?

There's no reason why you couldn't work out which notes to play using your ears. However, having a bit of theory and advice on where to find these magical notes is always helpful. If the thought of theory scares you off, just do what you can and take your time. Music theory is usually simpler than most people think.

For this exercise and warm up, we'll be working in the key D major. In other words, we'll be using a bunch of chords and notes that sound good with D. In any key, you have a whole host of notes at your disposal that you can use in any way and any order from the relevant scale. In this case, that scale is D major. For those of you who want to know, D major = D–E–F♯–G–A–B–C♯. Most guitarists learn scales in shapes, and these shapes are all over the fretboard, so the notes in D major will be everywhere you look.

Here's a diagram of all the notes from the D major scale. Use this to experiment with tapping melodies in this key. Find the patterns, recognize shapes you already know, and just marvel at how many options you now have with so many notes (and, of course, an extra hand!).

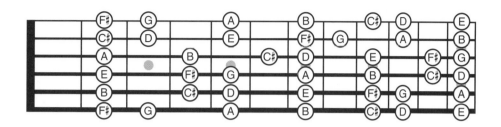

THE EXERCISE

It's well worth taking your time to compare the notes in the tab with the ones on the fretboard diagram above, as this will aid in your musical note understanding. The melody uses a lot of slides, so it's an ideal opportunity to try sliding to one of your own notes chosen from the fretboard diagram.

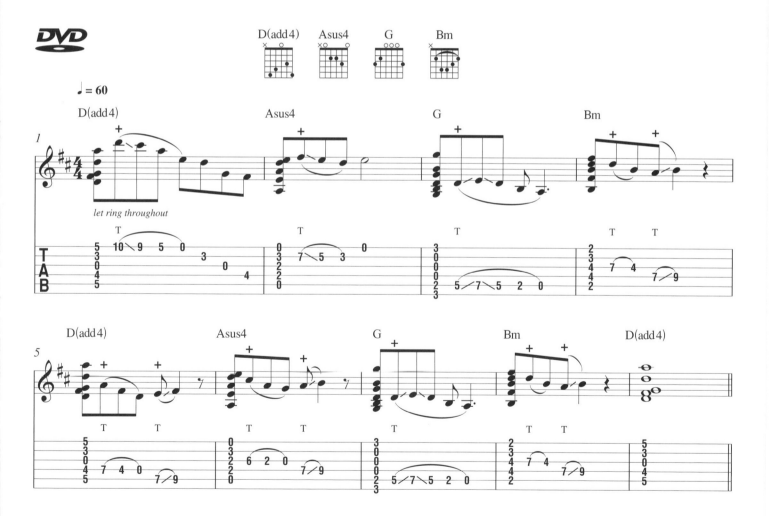

Finding Them in E Minor

THE WARM UP

This time we're working in the key of E minor. The principle is exactly the same as the previous exercise. We are using chords that work with E minor, and we have all the notes in the E minor scale at our disposal: E–F#–G–A–B–C–D. Try experimenting with the notes from the following diagram.

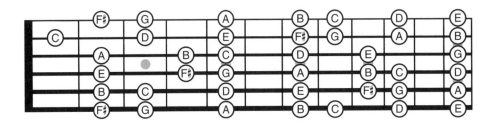

THE EXERCISE

This one has got quite a fiery feel to it. Really try to lock into the rhythmic repeated patterns and work on making them as powerful as possible. Try experimenting with the melodic phrases that appear with chords Am and C, using the diagram from the warm up. Remember to hold the chord throughout the bar.

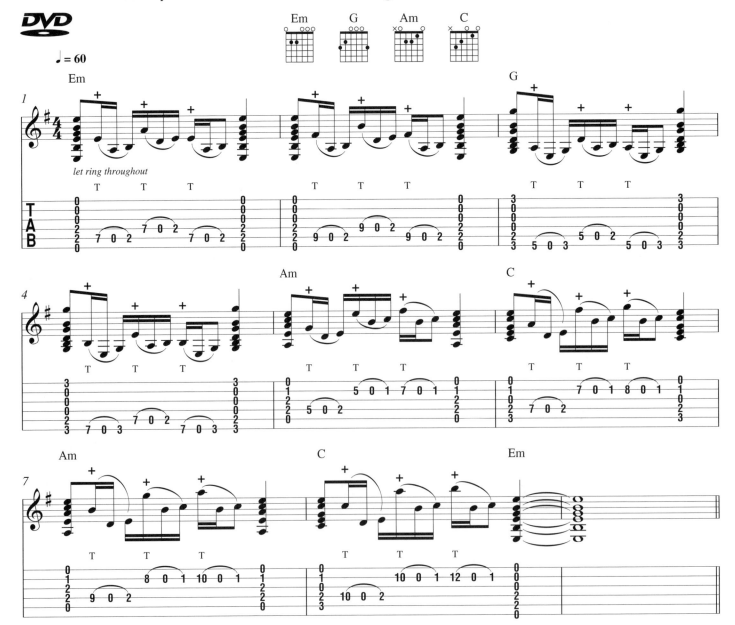

Double Fingers

THE WARM UP

Using two fingers for tapping can even further expand your playing. You can now play some really interesting intervals; you can even add more fingers and actually tap out chords. For now, just add an extra finger; if you are using your middle finger, simply add your index.

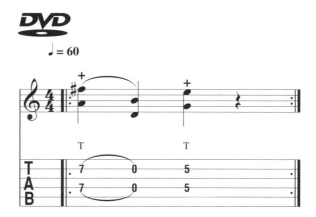

THE EXERCISE

There are no major surprises here; just play it slowly and focus on getting the notes even. Notice how closely the left and right hands are working together. Once it becomes natural, you should start to feel as though you are playing a piano, literally bouncing around the fretboard.

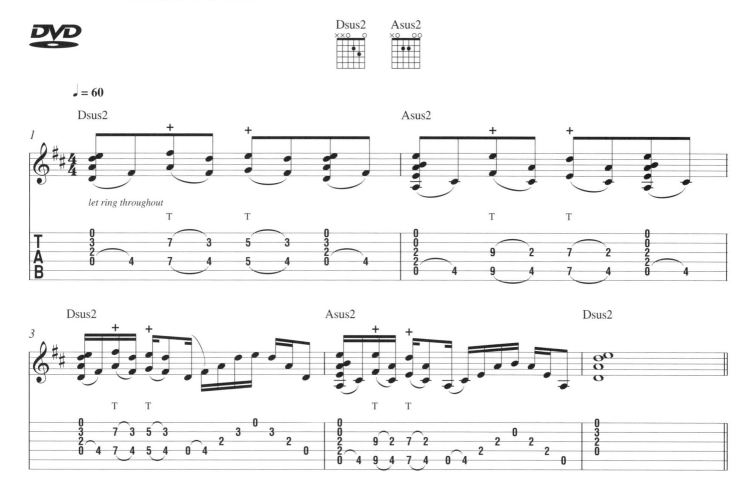

Double Stops

THE WARM UP

Some people attempt tapped double stops (two adjacent strings, played together) with two fingers, but they are easily—and perhaps better played—with one finger. Use this warm up to get used to this new technique. If you are using one finger (most likely to be your index finger), notice how you need to bend your finger backwards slightly, focusing the pressure towards the fingertip to avoid playing all six strings.

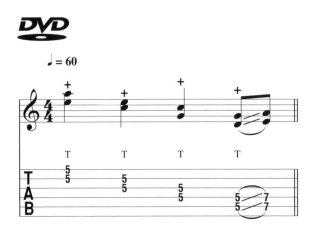

THE EXERCISE

The only real surprise here is that you are pulling off in bars 2 and 4. Hold each chord for the whole bar to get a fuller sound.

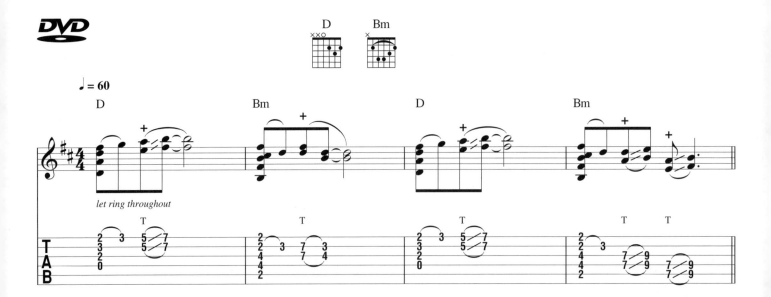

CHAPTER 4: Harmonics

Harmonics are magical things. They create that classic bell-like chime. Very simply put, harmonics are best explained as a note divided. It's a bit strange to think a note can be sliced in half or chopped into quarters, but it can. When we play a note on the guitar, such as an open E, we think we hear only one sound. In truth, we are hearing that E note and a whole bunch of other, higher notes (albeit much fainter) mixed together. A harmonic actually separates those notes, which creates the ethereal and alien sound. They really work well amongst the other percussive techniques, as well.

Keeping It Natural

THE WARM UP

Creating a harmonic—or, in this case, a natural harmonic—is a bit tricky at first. Lightly touch the string (don't press down) over the relevant fret (directly over the fret wire) and strike the string. Two questions (the "two P's") are worth keeping in mind when learning to play harmonics: position (i.e., where are you exactly on the fretboard?) and pressure (i.e., how much pressure exactly are you applying?). This warm up will help you explore most of the natural harmonics that are relatively easily achievable; you'll no doubt find the 12th fret the easiest. Take note of the melodies that can be created simply by working up and down the strings at various fret locations.

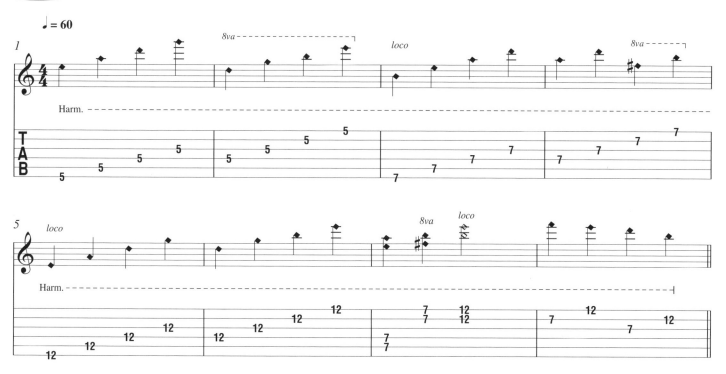

THE EXERCISE

BARS 1–2: Here we are playing a harmonics-based melody; the harmonic on fret 5 will be the hardest, so just take your time.

BAR 3: This is more of a chordal sound. Again, spend time to make sure the fret 5 harmonic rings out clearly.

BAR 4: Here we have a short, but fairly fast run. If you make sure all the notes are left ringing, it should sound magical.

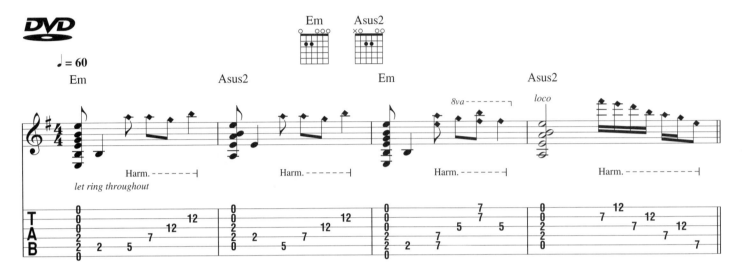

Slapped Harmonics

THE WARM UP

Use your pick-hand's middle finger (pointing downwards) to slap against the relevant fret. Position is once again very important; you must be exactly over the fret wire. Slap the strings enough to make them seemingly bounce against the fret wire, with most of the movement coming from your wrist. Once you have a good sound, start focusing on isolating the three strings that are tabbed out. Don't worry too much about this, though, as any extra strings will just add to the percussive quality.

After you've mastered hitting several strings, try slapping just one string by angling your hand and finger (similar to how you would tap a note, but remember to bounce off the string).

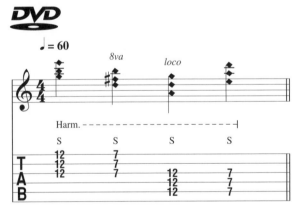

THE EXERCISE

Notice in the following exercise how the number of strings we're slapping varies. This is simply because we are holding the chord for the whole bar to add to the overall sound, and only the open notes will ring out as harmonics. (But don't be afraid of hitting the other strings.) Keep adjusting how many you hit until you get the best sound—one which is full and where the harmonics aren't overpowered.

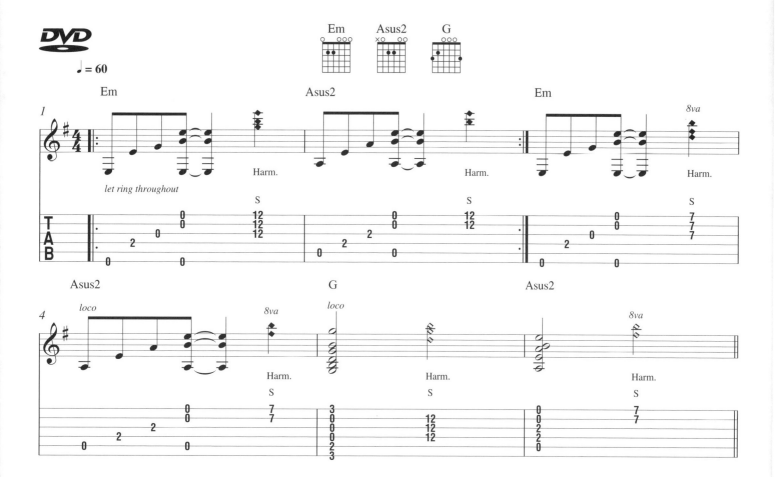

Artificial Slapped Harmonics

THE WARM UP

It sounds serious, doesn't it? But don't worry; it's really not that much different! An artificial harmonic is one that involves fretted notes instead of open strings. We do this by playing a harmonic 12 frets above our fretted note. (It will work in other divisions too, but we'll keep it simple for now.)

We can play artificial harmonics in a variety of ways, but this time we are sticking to slapping (remember, you can slap several notes or individual notes by simply angling your hand). The tablature indicates where to slap with your picking hand (the tab numbers in parentheses); your fretting hand will be fretting notes 12 frets below this, which is also shown in the tab. For example, for our second group of notes, we fret notes at the 2nd fret and slap the harmonics on the 14th fret. The artificial harmonics are indicated by "A.H." in the music.

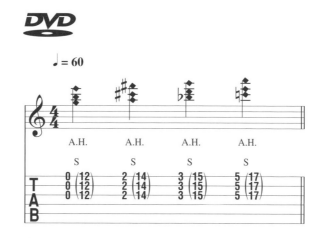

THE EXERCISE

We're using barre chords in this example, so pay attention to how the left and right hands have to move in concert to achieve the various harmonics. For example, when you play a G barre chord, your fingers shift up to third position, and your picking hand has to travel the same distance when playing the harmonics. This will help the movement become much more natural and coordinated.

A More Traditional Approach to Artificial Harmonics

THE WARM UP

This time we're playing artificial harmonics in the more standard way, which involves using your thumb and finger at the same time. These are also referred to as "harp harmonics," and we'll soon discover why. Note that these harmonics are indicated with "H.H." in the music.

BARS 1–3: We are just using open strings to make it easier for you (so essentially using the artificial harmonics technique to play natural harmonics). Rest the first finger (of your picking hand) over the 12th fret, just like you would for a natural harmonic, but using the opposite hand, and then use your thumb to pluck the string downwards. (Alternatively, you can use the third finger of your pick hand to pluck the string upwards.) Your finger should be at a 45-degree angle to your thumb and completely straight. Make sure your finger stays perfectly still until you pluck the string, then move it away to give the string room to vibrate. As with the first exercise in this chapter, keep in mind position and pressure.

BARS 4–6: It's slightly more challenging here, as we are moving up the neck to get harmonics on each note of an E minor chord.

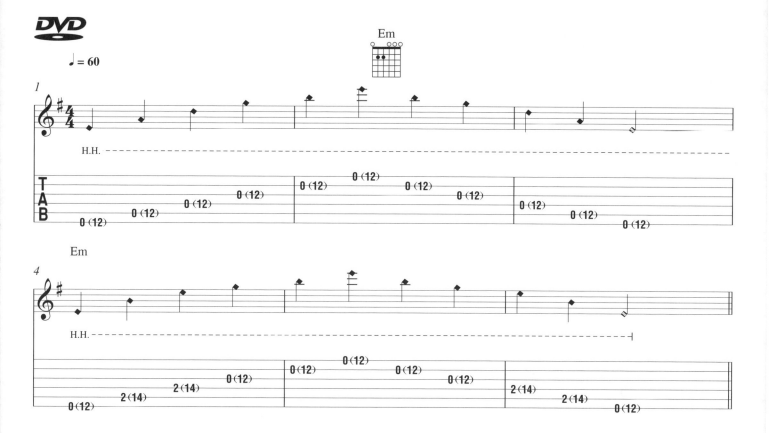

THE EXERCISE

Give the chord at the beginning of the bar a heavy strum and then take your time picking through the artificial harmonics (while still holding the chord of course!). Bars 3 and 4 are very similar, but we've squeezed in double the amount of artificial harmonics. Once you get into a flowing motion, this will be much easier, so stay relaxed and never rush things.

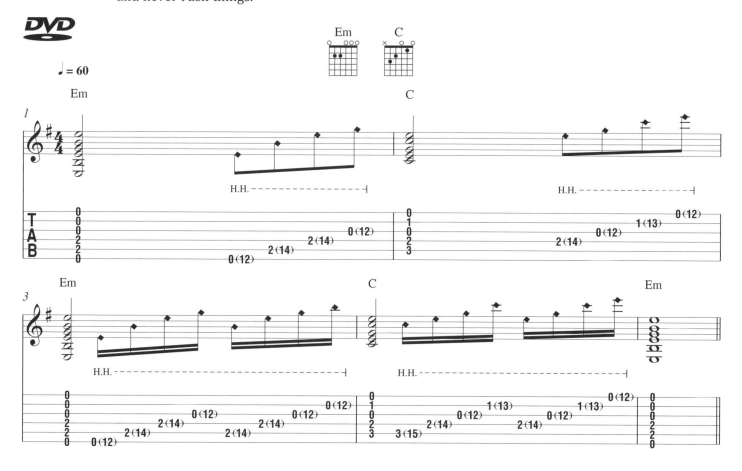

Percussive Acoustic Guitar   **41**

Making It Melodic

THE WARM UP

Up until now, all our artificial harmonics have been based around chords. Now we're simply using the technique to play single notes in a melodic way. Easy!

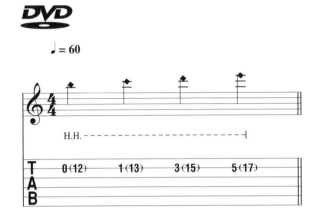

THE EXERCISE

This exercise mixes chords with melody; take some time to look through the tab and notice when the chord becomes melody (usually about beat 3), so you can plan ahead. If you can hold the chord while playing the melody, it will help create a fuller sound.

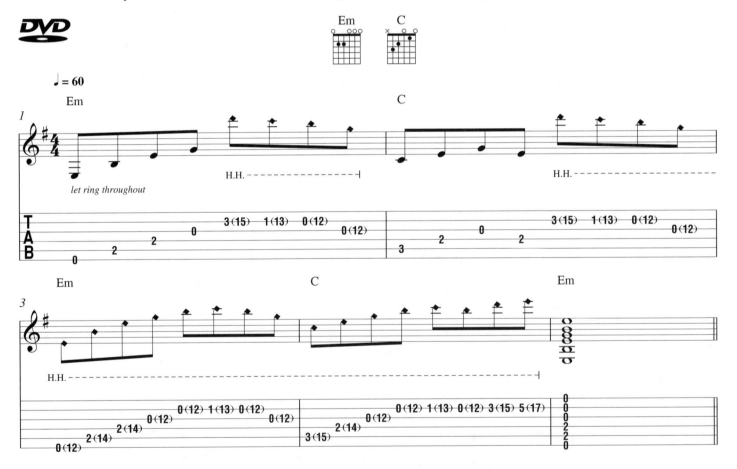

Harping

THE WARM UP

This technique sounds simply stunning. We are mimicking the sound of a harp by mixing standard notes with artificial harmonics. You should use your third or second finger to pluck the standard note. Be sure to practice this slowly and allow all the notes to ring together; the key to getting a harp sound is to get the notes evenly spaced.

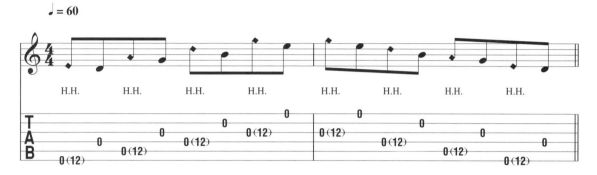

THE EXERCISE

The main thing to be aware of here is that, with the obvious exception of the last bar, we are harping throughout, so every other note is an artificial harmonic. Hold the relevant chord throughout the whole bar, keep it steady, and enjoy the sound it creates. This technique can also be played in an ascending direction by playing the harmonic with your third finger and the standard note with your thumb.

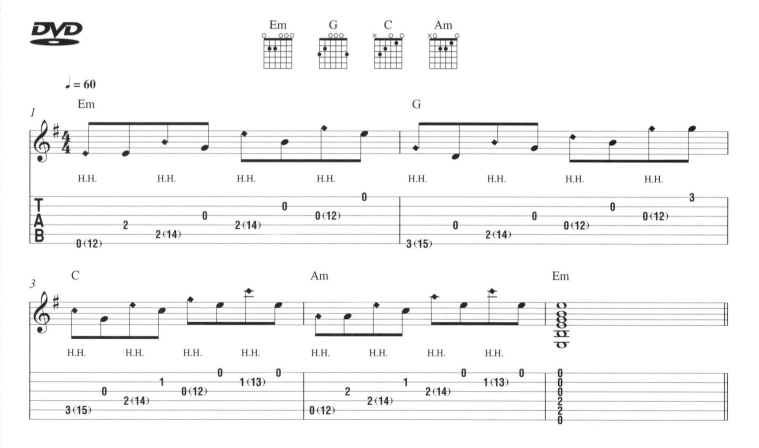

CHAPTER 5: Alternate Tunings

The subject of alternate tunings has been saved until last. Why? Well, it will completely change the way you approach your instrument. It's important to understand that your guitar doesn't have to be tuned the way we have come to believe is "standard." The most basic string alterations will completely change the way the guitar sounds. And, of course, all your scale patterns get jumbled up. To some, this might seem scary, but to others, it's a great way of giving you a fresh approach to the guitar. With many tunings, you also free your hands up to concentrate on creating other sounds—like body percussion for example—as the sound of open strings is deeper and fuller.

The following examples will give you a good grasp of the subject, but don't forget there are endless ways to tune your guitar. Refer back to the Introduction for more inspiration, and don't forget to try creating your own tunings!

☞ **TIP:** Although we have supplied instructions on how to reach these new tunings, it's worth purchasing an electric chromatic tuner, as it really will make your life easier!

Drop D Tuning

THE WARM UP

Drop your low E string down to a D. It's an easy thing to do, it won't confuse the fretboard too much, and now you have the full power of a low D to play with. In this warm up, we're simply working through some chord shapes in D major, with the drop D plodding away in support. If you haven't got a chromatic tuner, simply use your open D string (string 4) as a tuning reference.

Drop D tuning:
(low to high) D-A-D-G-B-E

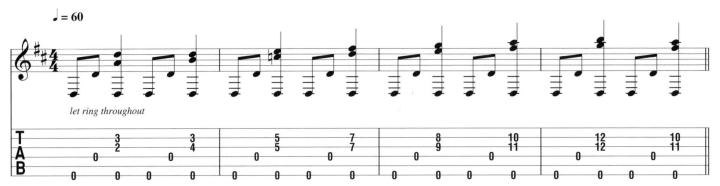

THE EXERCISE

BARS 1–2: We are using the drop D beneath simple melodies here. Let the drop D ring out and notice how much it adds to the accompanying notes.

BARS 3–4: Now introducing the idea of a constant bass part, we are simply alternating the drop D and the higher D string and then throwing in the melody from the first two bars.

BARS 5–6: These final two bars are basically an arpeggio; be aware of how we accelerate to 16th notes in beats 3 and 4.

Drop D tuning:
(low to high) D-A-D-G-B-E

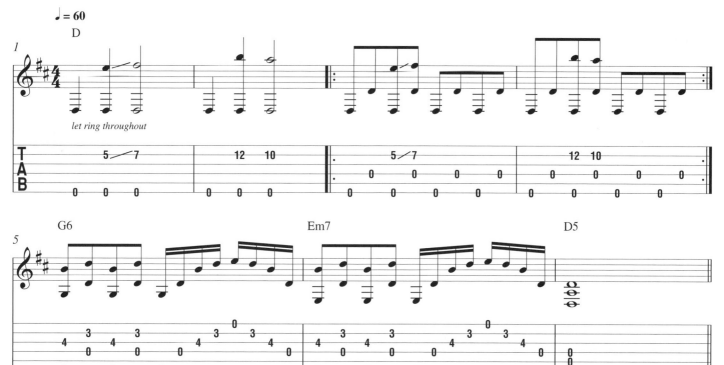

Drop C Tuning

THE WARM UP

We are now taking our lowest string even lower to the dark depths of C! You should notice how the string is now much more slack than before—so much so that you might even have a bit of a buzzing sound when you fret a note. If you palm mute this string (simply dampen the string with your palm) and pluck with a lot of attack, you will get a great percussive bass sound. Experiment with how much you mute the note to get the best sound possible. Be sure to kill each note after you have played it to add to the percussive feel. The rhythm might look a little daunting, but remember it's just another repeated pattern. You can use the 3rd fret on the A string as your tuning reference here.

Drop C tuning:
(low to high) C-A-D-G-B-E

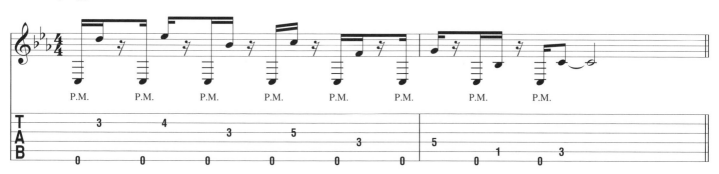

THE EXERCISE

The riff in the first bar should be the only real challenge here if you have spent enough time on the warm up. The rest is essentially the warm up repeated. Concentrate on perfecting your percussive sound while picking the drop C string.

Drop C tuning:
(low to high) C-A-D-G-B-E

DADGAD Tuning

THE WARM UP

DADGAD is one of the most well-known alternate tunings. When strummed open, the strings create a Dsus4 chord, which is why it has such an addictive and open sound. DADGAD lends itself to using the techniques that really make use of the open strings.

Use other open strings as reference for tuning—e.g., tune your high E string (string 1) to the sound of your D string (string 4).

BAR 1: Here we're mixing an octave (the two fretted notes) with open strings; simply strum the chord shapes, and enjoy how effortless it is to create such an amazing sound!

BARS 2–3: We're hammering on notes with open strings played on either side, creating a harp-like sound.

DADGAD tuning:
(low to high) D-A-D-G-A-D

THE EXERCISE

All the chords in this example are based around their more basic relatives. For example, our Gadd9 is essentially a G chord, but the addition of the open notes has added a whole new dimension. Once you've mastered this exercise, try creating your own chords. One- or two-fingered chord shapes often sound the best; just let the new tuning do the work for you.

DADGAD tuning:
(low to high) D-A-D-G-A-D

CGCGCD Tuning

THE WARM UP

This is a wonderful tuning. It's lower than DADGAD and has a slightly different character. The strings are tuned in such a uniformed pattern that you can play runs or melodies across the strings, repeating them in each octave without really having to change position. The feel of having such slackened strings can really change the way you play and help create new and exciting ideas.

If tuning from standard, tune your high E (1st string) down to D using the 4th string as a reference. Then tune your B string (2nd string) up to C using the 3rd fret of the A string (5th string). Then tune the remaining 6th and 4th strings to C. Finally, tune your 5th string down to G using your 3rd string as a reference. You could also think of this as Csus2 tuning.

Csus2 tuning:
(low to high) C-G-C-G-C-D

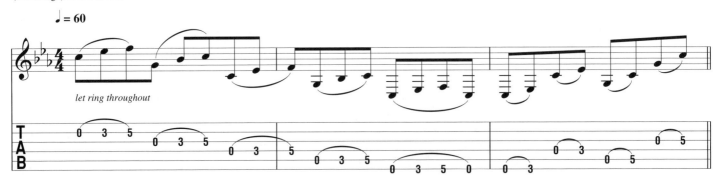

THE EXERCISE

Master bars 1 and 2 and you will sail through the rest of the exercise. The rhythm is the key here; notice the groovy feel in bar 1 and the equally spaced notes in bar 2. Once you have a good feel for those bars, move on. You can then pay attention to the rhythm and patterns that are introduced in bars 3, 5, and 7.

Csus2 tuning:
(low to high) C-G-C-G-C-D

Octaves and Intervals

THE WARM UP

We are staying in CGCGCD here, but now focusing on octave playing and exploring the fretboard. Playing melodies with an octave (an accompanying note a register higher) in an alternate tuning sounds fantastic and can really help you come to grips with the fretboard in a new tuning. By coming back to open notes as a reference point, you can quickly find new undiscovered harmonies.

Csus2 tuning:
(low to high) C-G-C-G-C-D

THE EXERCISE

This is the same groove-based idea from the previous exercise, but we're now introducing basic melodies created from the notes in the warm up. You should feel confident in no time, and once you do, start making it your own and rearrange those notes. Why not even try to add some of the techniques from previous chapters?

CHAPTER 6: Pulling It All Together

Rural Sun Rise

This piece is written in DADGAD and is inspired by the Celtic style of acoustic playing. It blends a range of the techniques from throughout this book, including some tricky string slaps near the end. The body percussion is focused around the top part of the guitar, so it may be worth referring to the Moving Up section of the Body Percussion chapter to refresh your memory.

Percussive Acoustic Guitar

53

Holiday to Spain

As you probably guessed by the title, this piece is Spanish-influenced, mainly drawing on flamenco music, but with a host of modern twists. The body percussion in this piece moves to two different areas of the guitar, and there are some tricky taps and pull-offs. Fortunately, you should find the harmonics in the outro fairly relaxing.

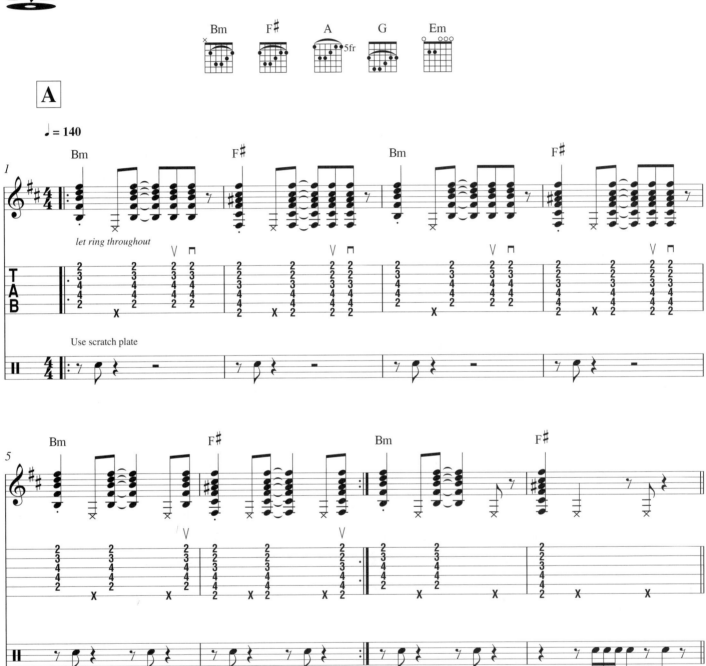

Percussive Acoustic Guitar

⊕ Coda

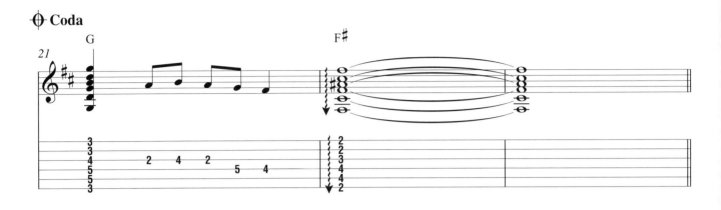

D

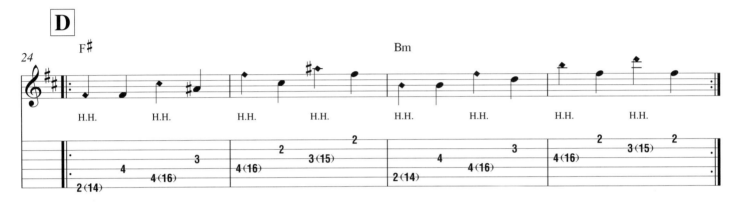

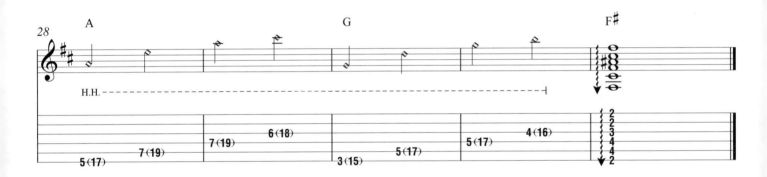

The Ballad of the Songsmith

This one is for the singer-songwriters. Written in drop D tuning, this ballad is addictively rhythmic and repetitive. The body percussion is based at the end of the guitar, except for the occasional fret hand snare sound. Concentrate on giving the groove a bouncy feel.

Drop D tuning:
(low to high) D-A-D-G-B-E

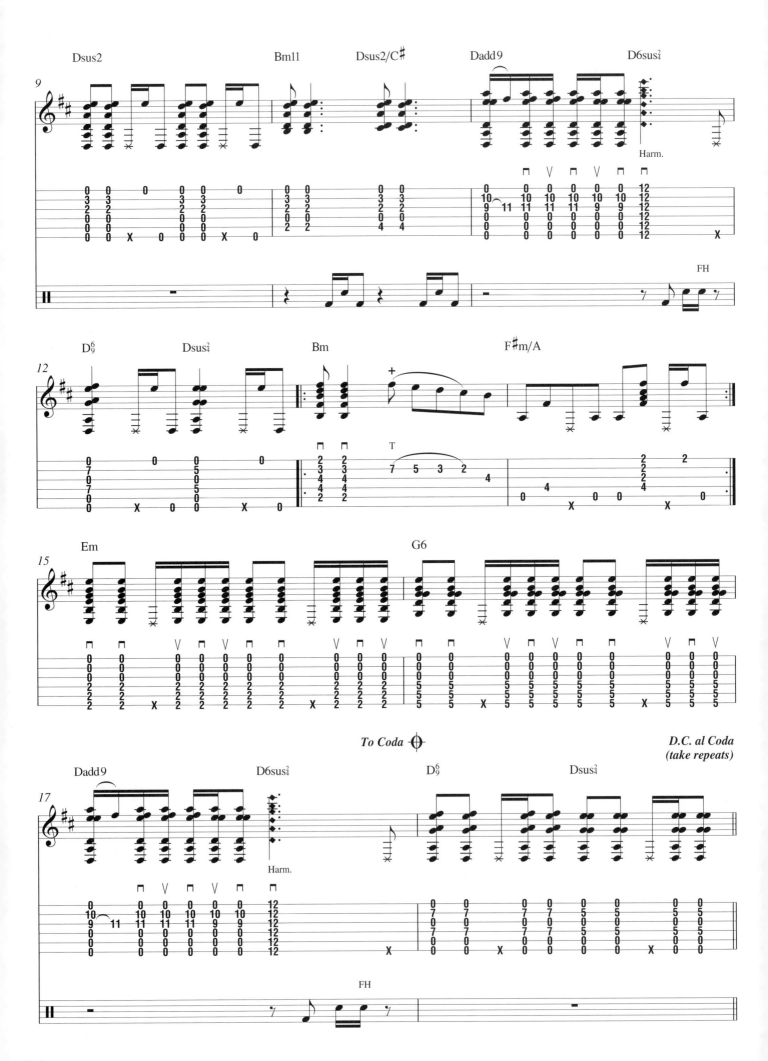

⊕ Coda

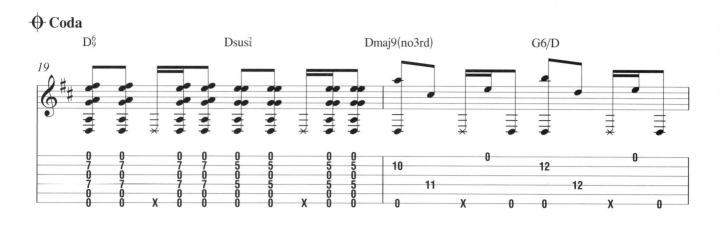

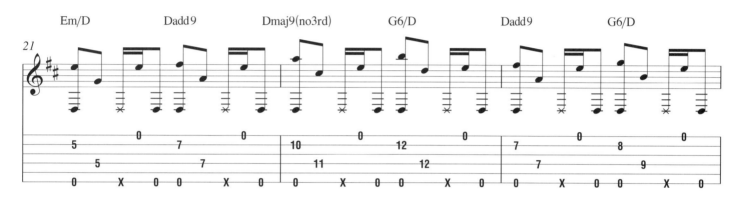

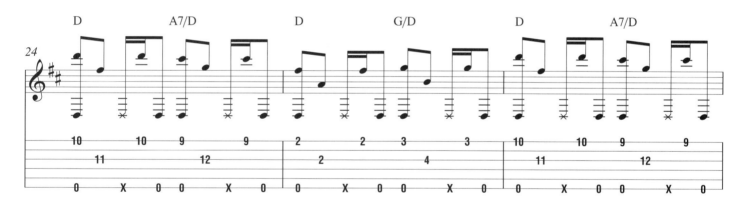

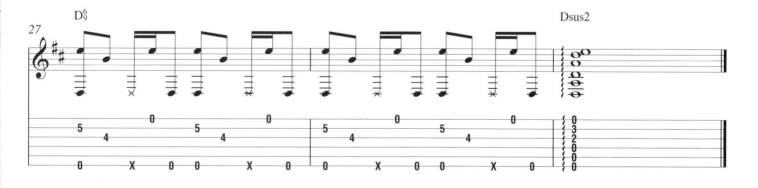

Slappin' the Funk

On first inspection, the rhythm might look daunting. Trust me, though; it's a very familiar feel. It only looks scary because there are so many short, syncopated notes and rests. These offbeat, short notes and rests are the key to getting the funk, so be sure to use your fret hand muting to create a crisp, funky sound. The majority of the notes are slapped, so make sure you are comfortable with both string slaps and the slap bass style. The body percussion hits are focused on the end of the guitar, but keep your eyes open for fret hand hits!

Csus2 tuning:
(low to high) C-G-C-G-C-D

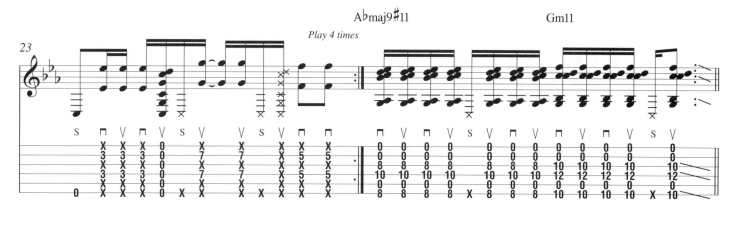

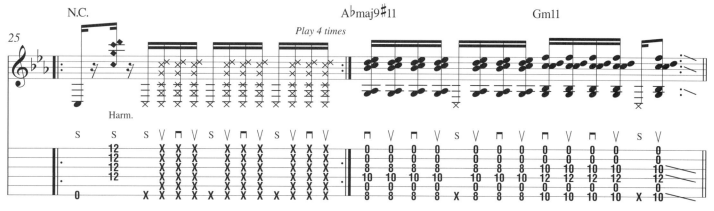

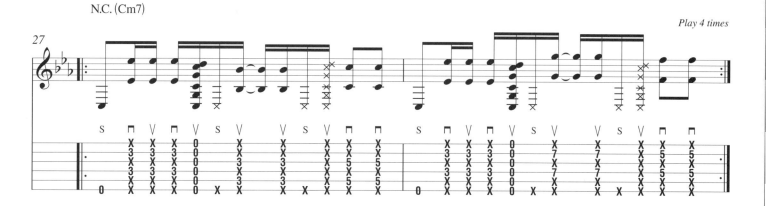

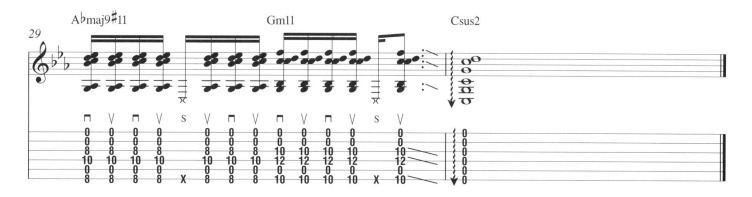

EXPAND YOUR ACOUSTIC GUITAR KNOWLEDGE

THE HAL LEONARD ACOUSTIC GUITAR METHOD
INCLUDES TAB

by Chad Johnson

This method uses real songs to teach you all the basics of acoustic guitar in the style of the Beatles, Eric Clapton, John Mellencamp, James Taylor and many others. Lessons include: strumming; fingerpicking; using a capo; open tunings; folk, country & bluegrass styles; acoustic blues; acoustic rock; and more.

00697347 Book/CD Pack..............................$16.95

DVD ACOUSTIC GUITAR
DVD   INCLUDES TAB

Acoustic Guitar – At a Glance features four lessons, including: Strumming Chords, Fingerstyle Basics, Travis Picking, and Capo Basics and uses the riffs of 16 songs, including: Brown Eyed Girl • Dust in the Wind • Free Fallin' • Landslide • Maggie May • Norwegian Wood (This Bird Has Flown) • Yesterday • and more.

00696017 Book/DVD Pack $9.99

ACOUSTIC GUITAR CHORDS
DVD

by Chad Johnson

Acoustic Guitar Chords teaches you the must-know chords that will get you strumming quickly. The included DVD demonstrates each chord and all the examples are accompanied by a full band, so you can hear these chords in the proper context. Teaches: open chords, barre chords, seventh chords, other chord types (suspended, add9), open-string drone chords, full song examples, and more.

00696484 Book/DVD Pack $9.99

HAL LEONARD BLUEGRASS GUITAR METHOD

by Fred Sokolow

This book uses popular bluegrass songs to teach you the basics of rhythm and lead playing in the styles of Doc Watson, Tony Rice, Maybelle Carter, Lester Flatt, and many others. Lessons include Carter strumming, alternating bass, waltz strums, using the capo, hammer-ons, pull-offs, slides, crosspicking, and much more. Songs include: Amazing Grace • Blue Moon of Kentucky • Cripple Creek • I Am a Man of Constant Sorrow • I'll Fly Away • We'll Meet Again Sweetheart • The Wreck of the Old '97 • and more.

00697405 Book/CD Pack..............................$16.99

HAL LEONARD FINGERSTYLE GUITAR METHOD
INCLUDES TAB

by Chad Johnson

The *Hal Leonard Fingerstyle Guitar Method* is your complete guide to learning fingerstyle guitar. Songs covered include: Annie's Song • Blowin' in the Wind • Dust in the Wind • Fire and Rain • Georgia on My Mind • Imagine • Landslide • Tears in Heaven • What a Wonderful World • Yesterday • You've Got a Friend • and more.

00697378 Book/CD Pack..............................$17.99

HAL LEONARD FOLK GUITAR METHOD
INCLUDES TAB

by Fred Sokolow

You'll learn: basic strumming; strumming variations; Carter-style flatpicking; bass runs; basic fingerstyle patterns; alternating thumb patterns; flatpicking solos; hammer-ons and pull-offs; fingerpicking solos; using a capo; I-IV-V chord families; and much more. Songs include: Blowin' in the Wind • Freight Train • The House of the Rising Sun • Leaving on a Jet Plane • This Land Is Your Land • and more.

00697414 Book/CD Pack..............................$14.99

FRETBOARD ROADMAPS – BLUEGRASS AND FOLK GUITAR
INCLUDES TAB

by Fred Sokolow

This book/CD pack will have you playing lead and rhythm anywhere on the fretboard, in any key. You'll learn chord-based licks, moveable major and blues scales, major pentatonic "sliding scales," first-position major scales, and moveable-position major scales. The book includes easy-to-follow diagrams and instructions for beginning, intermediate and advanced players. The CD includes 41 demonstration tracks to help you perfect your new skills.

00695355 Book/CD Pack..............................$14.99

HAL•LEONARD®

7777 W. BLUEMOUND RD. P.O. BOX 13819
MILWAUKEE, WISCONSIN 53213

www.halleonard.com

Prices, contents, and availability subject to change without notice.

FRETBOARD ROADMAPS FOR ACOUSTIC GUITAR
INCLUDES TAB

by Fred Sokolow

Learn to play lead, rhythm, chords & progressions anywhere on the fretboard, in any key and in a variety of styles. Each chapter presents a pattern and shows how to use it, along with playing tips and guitar insights. For beginning to advanced players, with a CD featuring demos of all the exercises, plus practice tracks to help you learn six different soloing techniques.

00695940 Book/CD Pack..............................$14.95

 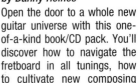

MASTERING ALTERNATE TUNINGS
INCLUDES TAB

by Danny Heines

Open the door to a whole new guitar universe with this one-of-a-kind book/CD pack. You'll discover how to navigate the fretboard in all tunings, how to cultivate new composing and improvising concepts, and how to broaden your fingerstyle skills and techniques. The CD includes 40 tracks for demo and play-along.

00695787 Book/CD Pack..............................$19.95

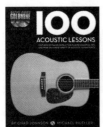 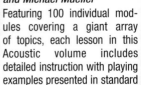

100 ACOUSTIC LESSONS
INCLUDES TAB

by Chad Johnson and Michael Mueller

Featuring 100 individual modules covering a giant array of topics, each lesson in this Acoustic volume includes detailed instruction with playing examples presented in standard notation and tablature. You'll also get extremely useful tips, scale diagrams, chord grids, photos, and more to reinforce your learning experience, plus 2 full audio CDs featuring performance demos of all the examples in the book!

00696456 Book/2-CD Pack..............................$24.99

PERCUSSIVE ACOUSTIC GUITAR METHOD
DVD   INCLUDES TAB

by Chris Woods

Providing detailed, step-by-step instruction on a variety of percussive guitar techniques, this book includes warm-ups, exercises, full peices, and pracitcal "how-to" training that will get you slapping, tapping, and enjoying your guitar like never before. Covers: string slapping, body percussion, tapping, harmonics, alternate tunings, standard notation and tab, and more!

00696643 Book/DVD Pack..............................$19.99

TOTAL ACOUSTIC GUITAR
INCLUDES TAB

by Andrew DuBrock

Packed with tons of examples and audio demonstrations, this book/CD package breaks down the most common, essential acoustic techniques with clear, concise instruction and then applies them to real-world musical riffs, licks, and songs. You'll learn syncopation, power chords, arpeggios, rhythm fills, and much more.

00696072 Book/CD Pack..............................$19.99

0313